Subterranean Hum

Peter Case and David Ensminger

"EVERY HUNDRED FEET THE WORLD CHANGES."
– Roberto Bolano

DAVID ENSMINGER

1980s – 2014

Lexicon Blues

My language is not pork chops or brown gravy or chicken flopped
   on a rusted grill or tainted wine or McDonalds or Taco Bell
My language is not a symbol of darkness, not a coiled snake, not
   a bleeding cross, not an eye droop, not a ceiling with neon
   swastikas
My language is not anymore obscure than a train rumbling
   through the sad yellow earth with its two eyes staring straight
My language is not Rilke's green tiger walking wounded behind
   his cage with a trickle of blood dried on his stunted claw
My language is not Chrysler, money-yielding dividends, or the
   American dream meeting layoffs and invalid insurance cards
My language is not some carol sung by the strange middle-class
   kids with pickpocket eyes faces shimmering in the 27-degree
   dinnertime Midwest
My language is not a long blues wail culled from Billy Holiday or
   Junior Wells, my color resembles London or Frankfurt, not
   Cairo Lima or Tokyo
My language is not a gutter in sleazy side Rockford, not a broken
   down refrigerator on 7th street, not a roach in Chinese food
   on Broadway, not a yawn in the ranch homes of Machesney
   Park
My language isn't scalded by high temperatures or insulated like a
   bruised orange, injured and bacterial, thrown away in a nest of
   white worms
My language comes from the land of tanks, napalm, B-52s, and
   Los Alamos
My language was in Watts and Chicago and Kansas and John
   Brown even used it Walt Whitman and John Reed
My language is buried beneath the Kremlin, kept in Utah salt
   mines, floating off the Georgia coast, and playing chess in
   Yugoslavia.

In the Shadow of Prevert

The air closed around us.
Sunlight kicked at our feet.
In the alley, a child bit a
dandelion, letting its milk
fall to a gray puddle.
It was then I loved you.

Haiku #1

burnt amber leaves fall
against the earth's skin
like flecks of oil
on a shimmering pond

Peepshow Dollars

headlights smear bartender streets
seashore slightly stirs canvas boats
devoid of daylight, a shack
sits astride the abandoned gas station

scrunched-up Kleenex
downcast eyes
blunt gossip in
elbow-to-elbow stalls

outside, trees sit naked
white with gull droppings
under the moon
of a disrupted October

men stretch condoms
taste cigarette mouths
entangled hairs
and perspiring loins

anxious fingers
cling to dilapidated paint
windows moisten
lips hang open

across from the derelict beach
where wives stand
under skinny umbrellas on
Saturday morning

Poem to Be Written in Chinese Letters

In the distance,
                  a hovering
                          murky glow.
Starving,
        unhappy,
   you chewed
        the sky
to bits.

        The glow remained.

Kenneth Patchen

Better to be
a butterfly with no wings
than a lizard
with an extra tongue

Haiku #2

broken teacups
lie sprinkled
across the ground
as if leaves
predicting winter

East 7th Street

nothing is true
except the body is dying

form to nada
anti-plastic

no silver
no steel

just an architecture of bones

full of tongues
shuddering in the night

Where the Gods Converge

the Gods converge here in March tumult,
preacher highway corridors,
Indian street food in dark glow storefronts,
a mix of sun splatter and freezing rain,
art deco 1929 malls, O. Henry's obscure plaque,
a paper factory endlessly leaking
a sarcophagus of smog

do you see

heirloom sheep in the shadows of Carl Sandburg's
books, "idiot box," and green viser,
leaf whirlwinds in front of black tunnels
punching through Cherokee territory

crystalline buildings in the new South
with the soul of a blue refrigerator
staring across heavy lines of piggybacking cars

the old dead textile mill offering hookahs
and chocolate martinis

outstretched in the last heave of winter
emaciated trees bend and creak
next to boarded-up houses, drainage ponds,
a cemetery with moss-eaten stones
leaning like feral sun dials,
and salt water pools in business hotels
serving Fruit Loops as health food

a hefty charcoal crow sits on the ledge
of a bank designed like a fast food joint
selling biscuit sandwiches
as bluegrass pours from the radio

pheasants walk crooked
alongside the shuttered
Blue Ridge highway

road failure keeps people
at fake Swiss chalets as
small town gas stations crumble next
to a library's fake Roman columns

a sunken football stadium stares at a cemetery
with Confederates graves marked with flimsy flags
and acres of flowers bright as Bakelite

we discover a company store, 1908,
shattered and roofless, scant
flaking remains of wallpaper filter
history's fading pigments

we walk the paths of King's Mountain
where wolves chewed on barely buried loyalists
after mountain men surged up soggy sides

the British captain was blown from his horse
as if a great wind pummeled him
others were hung from limbs
like silhouettes of human chrysalides

the elusive past converges
with Joan Jett airbrushed on a bathroom door,
comics glued to walls, and black-eyed pea tacos
the new South traffic curls up
towards an evangelical library
as dead Yankees lie massed in trenches
just beyond Amtrak's vein

the sound of God no more than
a whisper in Black Mountain's
bankrupt second hand store full
of rusted bullets and fossil clumps

Here Lies the Truth

They piled the old woman
in the leopard print coat onto the gurney
across the street in the pelting rain.
She seemed to squirm
like wet spaghetti
as gray sheets fell.

The old man at the video store
showed me new upper teeth
and swollen lip,
but his bottom teeth
remained distant and gapped,
as if in perpetual divorce.

The waitress at the diner
brought us cranberry juice
in a beer mug.

We could have slipped a quarter
in the game machine in the lobby,
tried to win a compact knife.

In the dark American-Irish pub
the only local joint giving customers
two-dollar bills as change for sour drinks

the one with lit-up
decorative stained glass,
European plate ware,
small press architecture
reviews complaining
about atomic age modernism,
and soft-focused antique pictures
of bygone families.

Peter sang unshackled
as mom and dads yapped
over wine in back
next to a mural
of a library shelf.

I walked home under limbs
dropping seed packs the size of baseballs.
Gazed at the polished floor
of the post office
and the fetid water trickling
from the burrito bar.

The air was cold and hard
a black cat scrunched up
against a lumber warehouse,
a kid tried to force open
a comic book shop door.

Reaching home amid a burping
heat blast, I flipped
on the television.

A man scrambled
through thriving streets of Yiddish
neon bagel wool suit New York City,
where men sold ties from a suitcase
propped up on the sidewalk.

Panicked and poisoned by failure,
he ran wounded
across the Williamsburg bridge,
the city like an insect
horde below him.

The vintage naked city of a million
stories erupted spellbound at two a.m.

The city of spells, broken car windows,
and the ghost of Walt Whitman.

No Horses In Sight

We ate Thai food until our eyes watered
underneath the elaborate chalk drawing
and tried to figure out the politics of
sex in America.

The store sold us an elephant
ornament made from candy wrappers tightly
twisted 3,200 miles away,
another put a white chocolate
morsel with pineapple butter
in a cellophane bag.
I flipped through mangled 45s
at the half-price joint,
endless no-names from DIY days
before digital democracy,
or brief moments of total stardom,
like Cindy Lauper's
queer friendly pop syrup.

The cold keeps us in bed for hours,
skin on skin, as the air cleaner
roars steady as a train.

Clothes hang from doors
and stair railings, a cup of soup awaits us.
I cleaned the tub and toilet wearing a beanie.
Somewhere in here is a Chekhov
story waiting to happen, I suppose.

In the meantime, I'll think about the Dutch
resistance in World War II, people's
fetish for stamps, the stars and moon
atop a rural bank building in Texas,
and the sound of the Buzzcocks.

If You Could Catch Butterflies

yesterday we talked shop about film noir
next to the overheated Xerox machine,
the room was rank and pungent with ink smell.

he told me about long two-person shots,
the art of limitations, off-screen deaths
conveyed by the stalled whir of an LP,
and the enduring stark shadows of Fritz Lang.

together we couldn't unpack memory --
who starred in *Cry of the City*, 1948, the
Italian cop and the framed thug?

everyone seemed to unleash a cacophony of wet
gurgling coughs around us, so I split to the
abandoned hospital waterfront with
a sun soaked gap-toothed façade

missing windows gulped the air.

pelicans dove endlessly,
plunging beaks into the morass of plastic
bags, rusted shopping carts, a rope
imitating a snake, and huge broken concrete.

a girl giggled, racing across the uneven parking
lot on a tricycle, three men hovered beneath
a makeshift umbrella, swallowing bagged beers.

a live oak twisted slowly, invisibly,
arms gnarled and majestic

next to erupting weeds

if you could catch butterflies
would you put them in here?

Keep Calm and Continue On

I scraped the last handful of gunked-up coins
from my green glass table in the shoe-lined
front room and walked to the taqueria with
the cheap happy hour.

Most of the way,
I worried about the coughing carburetors
of cars lining up to meet the freeway
and the steel sewer grate draining
into Galveston Bay.

I grabbed a water, handled the salsa bar
spoons gingerly with coarse bleached napkins,
and stared at my cue ball head in the bathroom,
trying to read every missing hair's story.

Turning around, I saw the sign flat on the wall.
"Keep Calm and Continue On."

Ants are climbing through my door
in a guerrilla war, the upstair's
sink has a deep and unsettling clog a day
after the landlord checklisted it as fine.

My wife's back erupts in spasms beneath soft
skin. The Presidential race has begun with
verbal sparring, but no one talks about
marijuana taxes as the Philippines absorbs
a hemorrhaging typhoon.

Last month a rock split my windshield
like a broken coconut,
another jetted under car, severing the heat
shield above my muffler.

But I can only think about watching
a beige small dog jump
onto the freeway's flat expanse,
jittery and confused by the concrete divider
and fleet of cars.

My stomach grew taut and sickened.
But then I was past the scene. I kept calm,
continued on, staring hard at the city's barely
visible exoskeleton, where people were
calculating the price of happiness.

The Flannel Moon Is Not Crashing
Through the Living Room Window

The flannel moon is not crashing
through the living room window
but the 'Ferrari of space' satellite
is horse-powering down
from the ceiling of the sky just
two weeks after Lou Reed died doing
tai-chi with eyes wide open
to the slanted light in his backyard.

I don't want to
hover on the irony.

Our love, meantime, seems to persist
effortlessly, moored to the original
combustion of that night when you stood
in the far corner of the bare concrete bar,
zoned in on my Doc Martens,
ignored the stains on my thrift store coat,
talked to me face-first about the blues,
and let me shadow you to the 24-hour
Mexican restaurant with the dripping
cheese plate, horchatas, and bags of water
to keep away bugs on the terrace
lit like a Christmas tree in August.

Even in the most monochrome days,
when we harvest the boredom of work
and wages in a city incubating NASA
and medical visions, even when others
surround us with Miller Light
and bad stories while bent over
on a 1940's bar, we glimmer
like throwbacks to a Cary Grant film.

Our love stems, perhaps, from such celluloid,
not coarse, loud, and tweeted from the bully pulpit
of a cellphone, but cast-iron in its own solitudes
and pleasures, as when we wrestle with maps
over dry wine and peppered salad, trying
to find the next invisible road to encounter,
the next piece of anachronistic architecture
to photograph because it is hand-built and
reminds us of our own history.

We may not have the nimble hands of celloists,
the shaking typhoons of daily heartbreak,
the Studebaker of paychecks, or even
the safety and performance of suburban make-believe,
but we have a red-dirt kind of honesty,
hands hungry to peel down jeans,
a smile not camera-ready as polished porcelain
but real as a welder's flare that blurs the world,
a smile that electrifies our bones and breaks
us from prison. It is our quiet anthem, played
at seven thousand revolutions a minute.

Stranded

rain, rain rain, each muddied drop
like a miniature deluge, Styrofoam
cups filling Goose Creek, the car
skimming down the road as if
Jesus in a hotrod crossing water.

rain rain rain the heavy nitrate
pond where the bulging water buries
cattails and weeds, the faces of the
women smeared, each man donning
a soaked baseball cap, chunks
of broken trees peppering every corner.

rain rain rain a yuppie
hitting my car from behind with a sheepish grin,
massive gusts marking the upheaval
of God-stuff, a Halloween sugar cookie
crumbling in my cloth bag, ants
milling in my keyboard slots.

rain rain rain the microwave is dead
the lease has run out, a painting just
hit the floor, a kid wants to hitch a ride
to England to discuss Plato and bondage.

rain rain rain Julie says her lunch tastes
like dirt my dad fumbles with the computer
I can't find my phone can't remember
to read Jack Spicer.

rain rain rain manhole covers
cough up gallons, squirrels look
glazed with Vaseline, I stuck
my glass in the fridge next
to old salsa and ketchup packets.

rain rain rain the costumes
of mice and men will be dark and damp
I don't understand the math of baseball
the legend of Lou Reed is
surrounded by feedback, S&M, red joysticks,
the gunk of New York City.

rain rain rain I can't sell
can't buy can't lie can't steal
can't bury the way I feel...

That Roar of Masses Could Be Art

the Mexican carnival unloaded
like wheeled Legos in slow motion
at the south mall as we ate watery
Thai food across the street next
the warehouse emblazoned
by ten-foot graffiti portraits
of Salvador Dali and Muhammad Ali.

HUD housing girls in crisp white T-shirts
walked by, dangling corner store bags,
a side-swiping wind blew American flags on
the Ferris wheel into combustible patterns,
a Toucan painted on the side
of a yellow truck said nothing.

We drove home as Harley bikers
kicked out a stiff leg, veered
near the walled embankment, and chased
each other between hordes of SUVs
headed to the stadium.

The neighborhood looked dazed
in the afternoon sun. A man held up a sign
sketched, "Do not steal, need a meal"
next to the place where waitresses
wore shorts no bigger than Friday night panties
under TVs blaring college football 'civil wars.'

A boy stomped on law books and vanilla
folders inside a rusted Dumpster.
Another poked out a car window
with a slim plastic gun
and shot the side of the post office.

Yesterday, Heidi Klum
dressed as a ragged old heiress
with sallow crumpled paper skin
for party kicks and a talk show icon
got his ear pierced live as millions
squirmed.

Birds canvassed the sky, settling
on light poles and the superhighway's rim.

My consciousness grew heavy
a bit, so I slept through dinner and woke
to a pasty, dismal light and a knock on the door.

"Hey man, can I borrow a wrench,
can I borrow a jumper cable?"

I smiled, trying my hardest.

Venus in Furs Ad Infinitum

Michael sent me the text

"Lou Reed is dead"
factual and devastating.

as my legs moved up the hill towards
the French place with open-faced
sandwiches.

The waiter dressed like Popeye,
another as a nightmarish ghoul.

I walked the state cemetery with my wife,
reading the headstones of French
17th century rotted teeth seamen.

Surrounded by water, they died of thirst.

Water dribbled in a fake streambed.
The sky shed an October light.

Earlier, for an hour,
under the official seal of Texas,
I explained punk's outsider dream
and blues-fed shotgun shack poetry.

I signed the poster of a woman in a
wheelchair, eyed a Thai food truck,
and watched as General Grant's life
and death still drew a crowd on the
other side of the tent.

We soon left for the flat highway,
past silent mannequins in sequins on curbs,
men rolling a muddy tarp in front of the
piñata store, and a kid with two dogs splashing
through gas station puddles.

That's when I played

"The cold black sea waits for me me me
the cold black sea waits forever."

Lou's voice sounded tender, plaintive.
I snapped a photo of a broken restroom,
bought dehydrated vegetables, slept
at a pit stop near the coal plant,
and kept that tune near me.

For three hours, we huddled
in a spinal column of endless traffic
as welders sparked on the overpass
and pissed drivers drove blindly
into marshy ditches.

This morning, I will admit, felt worthless.
The same highway called me to work.

Right near the Golden Corral and the auto
parts store, as the concrete rose a bit,
I saw an unearthed William Blake sun stir
hot and Herculean below a thick knot
of clouds, causing the light to ascend in
slivers as ramblin' hard-nosed "Street Hassle"
morphed into the lines "It's such a perfect day."

Two minutes later, refineries
and rusted barges filled the horizon.

The black sea rolled over me me me.

I Have Become the Regular

I died a bit this morning on a sip of water
sucked in the wrong tube during a sci-fi
B movie on cable, coughed all over the sink,
eyes red hot, chest spasming, brain thickened.

The morning light flared
in the distance above the post office parking ramp,
seeds fell from trees, and a wet mattress
sat propped up against a law office dumpster.

Yesterday the rejection letter came
quick and friendly, decisive and declarative.

Your stories can't sell enough books.

So, I trekked to work, where teenagers yelled
about future bionic husbands, vaginal canal germs,
and low paying jobs. One was busted by the cops
for a 12 year-old parking ticket, spent the night in jail,
sweating. Another is contagious, another
is prepping her one year-old for Halloween.

By noon, I left to find my lover in Doc Martens
and short sharp hair. On the highway,
a long squat truck sat jack-knifed,
kissing a crumpled black pick-up.

Cop car lights shimmered,
ricocheting like merry-go-round glares.

Rain deluged the skyline, each building
became a squiggle of running colors
in the windshield. John Doe and Paul Westerberg
outblasted the air-conditioning, each like Bukowski
disguised with guitar in calloused hands.

A Volkswagen, rumbling on death's door,
cut into my lane.

My wheels spun in a gray asphalt roulette game.

This is what I am telling you.

Abandon the Past at Your Own Peril

"Fuck the environment," said the kid
with a wispy goatee and baggy pants,
impressing the girl under the canopy
of trees at the college's side entrance.

"I've never heard a bug make a sound like that,"
she said, half-startled, then hiccupped.

The kid had stuck a cigarette's
glowing tip into some hapless creature.

The day melted into lavender.

I paced the concrete, gingerly, my leg
still ached where I punched it while drumming
a Minutemen tune. The bruise looked like
a war torn country – all different colors --
but every one of them ugly.

I kept asking myself, "Who were the Saxons?"
"Should I read more Frank O'Hara?"
"Why does a piano sound soothe me?"
When I was smaller and skinnier,
when the night sent me into shakes,
when the crickets fidgeted under the carpet,
and the dog peed in the laundry basket.

When I crouched in the hallway,
trying to make my insomnia go far away,
sometimes I would look over my shoulder,
past my brother's drawing of a ceramic jug,
past my sister's spoon collection,
past the wooden ledge that ripped
my head open during a pillow fight
on my birthday, when I received stitches

instead of Tonka trucks, and see the piano
next to the museum-stiff chair and huge
lacquered green record cabinet,
and feel betrayed.

Some slight sound could have changed everything.
Instead, the cicada buzzed in the front screen,
the clock ticked mercilessly,
and the neighbor's CB radio crackled
to unknown territories.

One night I stole my handicap uncle's
car, steered down the northern highway
with a car full of jazz-rock and headlights
bright as the moon on steroids.

Soon I climbed the roof and pointed
a fake rifle into the scrawny dirt trail woods.

Soon I fired a roman candle
into my neighbor's gutter. Bright sizzling
cascades rinsed through their dreams.

Soon I would write down maps,
grammar rules, and science hypotheses.

Even now, though, that piano looms,
refusing to budge.

Alone in the Night

I woke at 5:18 a.m. and quietly cleaned the linoleum,
porcelain, and eggshell colored tub.

The light at the post office parking garage buzzed,
something jumped on my roof and scuttled across,
a car barely noticed the stop sign below.

Sleep has not been kind to me these few weeks,
I thought, then entered the side room,
where I flicked through flimsy yellow pages
of vintage stamps, the sundry treasures
                          of a dead friend.

This way, I keep him alive between my fingers.

I sang yesterday in the strange glare
of a rare dry Southern afternoon.

Above me a network of gas pipes probed the air,
geometric and stone silent. I muddied
my feet, threw a dripping blanket
into the embankment, and left without telling
goodbye to the kid running away
                          to South Carolina.

Today I drove for hours, a bit numb
to the affects of jarring potholes, the feel of a soft taco,
and the dust-heaped video store with a
                          broken cash register.

At the corner, a Middle Eastern man jumped
out of the backseat of a Lexus. His son
screamed behind air-conditioned
windows at a covered woman, blasted through the red light,
and crashed into the metal gas pump guard
                          of a 7-11.

Blocks down, a women in thick layers of turquoise
colored sweatshirts, scarves, and hat waited
to cross the street next to the bulldozed
                              Mexican grocery store.

A group of fantasy gamers, dressed in Crayola colors,
took over a park where the wilted community garden yawned.
They clashed in choreographed gestures.

I tried to move the grocery cart with two locked wheels
at the giant outlet store. I felt guilt for being there,
hid my employee parking pass in the tray
                              with scratched CDs.

A woman sang a cabaret tune near a food truck
serving Korean bowls in the lot. This used to be
a 1930's apartment complex, not Art Deco,
but finely made, until people let in weeds and possums.

It rusted day by day in a succession of sepia Polaroids
flipped endlessly in a book simulating the decay of motion pictures.

Coming out with a bag bulging, I watched
the skies grow murky, muddied.

A rain squall scowled nearby,
the banter of rain grew dense.

I pointed the car home,
listened to the ricochets.

Made to be Broken

The men in yellow plastic jackets chopped
down one-third of the tree across from
my kitchen door.

The umbrella of leaves
used to shiver above the ponds
glowing with gasoline colors rippled
by ecstatic blackbirds and morning doves.

Yesterday someone dumped a box of shoes next
to my gate after jumping out the backdoor of the
sporting goods store.

The alarm kept Julie on edge, she throbbed
in the dim back room as I headed through
thick bends of traffic to the smell
of aerosol in the skate park where graffiteros
made bold sweeps next to the molasses
churning bayou and the three story
condos peeking at downtown.

Already I miss hunks of that tree.

Removing a section of its squid arms makes
it look like a modern sculpture, or injured in
some unknown war.

I flash back to my apartment in rust
city Rockford, the tilted house
where I planted carrots
behind the saggy porch.

Across the street stood a massive tree,
big as the moon, it seemed, in front
of the high school. The kind built in
Roman column style, everlasting and regal
for years, now just a remnant of lawsuits
and bureaucratic paperwork.

Pot grew wild in the basement,
bugs would cluster on kitchen tile until lights scattered
them in all directions. Stu fried bologna
on the gas stove, three guys broke
in above us, toppled a television down the stairs.

Sometimes we fetched Italian food
in aluminum take-out trays down the block,
sometimes motorcycles gasped in
the driveway. I once hid from my girlfriend.
As she peeked in the window,
I fell behind old books and scratched LPs.

Once my mother visited, sat with warm tea
in a musty chair, still called me baby boy.

Now I open the door, vent kitchen fumes,
and look across the street at wounded wood.

North 3rd Street #1

The prostitutes yank fire alarms
in our building to jump inside a few scant minutes
and escape the winter's lunar freeze
and stares of late night loitering Hasidim.

Ann frosts the windows white, the furnace
belches for hours. I live in the room
with no windows, just a picture of Bonnie and Clyde.

Water bugs crawl in from the hall, dotting the homemade
Russian constructivist mural in blue and gray.

Sometimes I hear Nancy ask the lesbian bartender
at 3 a.m., "Did I do OK?" after she tasted her
between the sheets.

Sometimes I sneak into Laura's room
and steal quarters from her disheveled bed
and eye her typed stories and underwear.

During the day the building is alive.

The second floor throbs with a suitcase factory.
The first floor smells like lard and brown beans.
Next door a Chinese firm spills a truckload
of meat into the street. The East River
looks sluggish and fat.

Near here Henry Miller once lived, Ramblin'
Jack Elliott too. Perhaps next to the Polish grocery
store with the giant walk-in freezer. Maybe next to
the disco ball bar, or the Puerto Rican taco stand
slash postal station.

Sometimes when I leave the subway
after the abrupt first stop on the L, walking up
from the rat scurrying, water dripping station,
I can smell the East Indian spice wholesaler that stretches
for an entire brick block.

Sometimes I watch a punk band play
feverish and free on a beer-flecked loading dock.

Sometimes I stare down from the roof
at a clump of bicycles on the corner,
eye the stars with a slight smile, or look at
the skyline of Manhattan blink a million times in the rain.

Sometimes I listen to Emmylou Harris in the dark,
or touch a girl's red hair between her long legs.

Not even a photograph could tell this story
as the front room windows provide a glimpse of the day,
enough to rise and retrace my steps.

The Way of the World

The day has shrunk down on my shoulders,
the washer and dryer emit mosquitoes that spiral slow.

The banana tree looks clogged with slow death.

Above me, the air goes from gray to charcoal,
four roach skeletons lie upturned near the plastic bin,
someone's yanked up the feral melon
                    that sat engorged next to ferns.

The gate screeches then slams, the whole building trembles,
someone walks by the bathroom window, hands clamping
a phone, eyeing my chest through smudged blinds.

I await two toilet papers rolls, a mildewed shower curtain,
uncapped tubes of creams for mystery splotches,
carpet covering boards that tilt and groan, and video
games pounding and shelling pixalated horrors next door.

Photos of blurred unknown families pile up on
the corner of my desk under the nose of a stuffed
elephant next to a Band-Aid box, 1984 fanzine,
                            and screwdriver.

Yesterday I touched the side of the hothouse at school,
fans whirred, birds looked puzzled at their reflections.

Behind me a fountain paid by Exxon rippled, somebody
slunk into the mail room. Now, Julie coughs, turns, throws
her phone on the desk piled with old books, wraps up
into the beige blanket, hides from the flu.

Tomorrow the sun will gasp again, we hope.
I have another inch of lukewarm water to finish.
A letter arrives from the veteran's hospital telling me German
prisoners planted trees in the lawn or died staring
                        at pictures of Red Skelton.

I look at Julie, her breaths grow even, steady, locomotive,
a car rumbles briefly, some toad chortles.

A siren is out there, in red pulses of light unseen.
This is the way of the world.

The Seed Bombers

Ode to the Waldport, Oregon Conscientious Objectors Camp

Roosevelt's boys shoved
            me in the blackout zone
a stretch of broken and cracked-tooth capes
where the surf foams
white as potato salad.

They told me to plant a million trees
because I refused to shave Hitler's
moustache with a bayonet.

For nine hours I bent down in
            the wind-whipped
wet earth,
Joe Hill's ghost whispers filled
my ears.
Five men died as the Mennonites
cooked up their salvation. Henry
      Miller sent a letter wondering
why we couldn't see literature
two inches from our faces.

England brooded when bombed,
the Navajo clicked codes and
waited for a victory pow wow,
Russia starved then pushed
towards Berlin with dirty resilience.

America's ticker tapes
and Broadway newsreels
stirred in the shadow
of atomic mushroom clouds.

I printed Patchen books
at night on the sly,
odes from the shy pornographer...

Hirohito was humbled
on an aircraft carrier
while I advanced
on San Francisco

let loose the literary lion that ate America.

The pale fists of Hitler still rattle
here and there
on furious soapboxes made of lies

But the roots of my trees remain,
I remain...

vigilant, hungry,

at war with war.

A Strange Sonata

the morning sky unlids weakly
bits of light ease along
the edges of pulled hush hush curtains.

Joan Crawford flips her Ford on the
black and white television winter sludge
after phone call anxiety.

I walk the sidewalk outside my door
trees scratch my head
with fingers grotesque in the shadows.

limp, dank, and disheveled banana leaves
lie throughout the courtyard
where a rigid chair stands
atop a removed tree stump

two boxes of tomato plants wither

the washing machine thumps for no reason

I use an old sock to clean counters,
make brown rice and squash fruit

this is my memento to ordinary calm
waiting for the day's devouring

The Human Fly

they called great-grandpa the human fly
she told me
after lugging two suitcases up groaning
stairs from 1923.

she opened them with breaths beating
like hummingbird wings

unveiling a musty straight-jacket small
enough to cocoon a 12 year old

magic wands corroded and verified
by use

cards tricks in envelopes that once knew
Green Bay before the Packers

a hanky, coins that slip
underneath each other,
a photo with grandpa chained to a board,
a sublime stoicism
chiseled every gray feature.

they called him
"Suicide"

he'd let cars hit him at 60 mph
get up, nonplussed,
wave to the crowd,
nothing but a day's work

or walk blindfolded
on Sullivan skyscrapers

fluid and fleet as a minnow.

I smiled
my mouth must have looked
like an unclosed zipper

envy almost broke my back

what could they nickname
my family...

collectors of misfit toys?

Civil War sergeants
dried goods store operators
slick sewing machine sellers
factory foremen of ripe fruit gum
in Chicago's gridiron loins

mentally marred ones too...

the human cocktail lounge
whose breath was like the underside of
a Lake Erie pontoon.

the human octopus
who liked to touch children
under the shadow of a Great Dane.

Johnny UFO --
aliens visited him in high school.

she showed me the honorary fireman's card
pulled off a few tricks

but I kept thinking

where was the magic
when I looked back
and found the root of
my existence in trailer parks
and hobby shops?

was it inside
the homemade Beatles tape
unspooled next to a toy brass canon
the only thing grandpa
left dad before
he met God

and God turned his cheek?

PETER CASE

12 midnight, Kennedy dead 50 years

on a black strip in the oozing rain
after show Sun Sessions Elvis on
Prescott to Flagstaff highway 169
then 17 north in the pitch dark
I get this feeling alone at night
going over mountains hypnotized
there's somebody else in the car
headlights a soft carpet to roll in
car wrecks & heart attacks versus
boogie woogie four on the floor
eight to the bar chewing cough drops
the phone don't work up here
neither do the stars beclouded
gas stop in Casa Grande outlaws
in hoodies smoking at the gas pumps
we all eye each other then look away
in another bleak men's toilet roar of
the hand-dryer a fucking jet this all
night store beautiful colorful untouched
rows & rows of poison & the its
back on the molasses highway north
got a six hour drive tomorrow guhnight.

By the freeway

4:32 a.m. Tucson AZ
Motel 6 room 122
trucks fly down HW 10
its cold my ankles itch
& I didn't even bother
    to unpack
channel changer glows
    in the dark
then I'm feeling
    for the light switch
my guitars loiter
    by the door
hoping to make a break

it's raining on the desert
in this town if it ain't neon lit
    it's abandoned
pretty girl in grey sweats
pink t & blond pony tail
with death's head
tattoo on her right arm
working in the kitchen

life, love & death
take your pick
I'm going home
San Francisco
    in 6 days.

High Desert

Coming down from Flagstaff
six thousand feet
Bumble Bee, Arizona
past Bloody Basin
& Horse Thieves Road
along the Carefree Highway
a cactus flips the bird
by Dead Man Wash & the
Armed Forces Career Center
also, the 2nd Amendment store:
"guns--ammo--accessories
buy--sell -trade"
"A Quality ChemDry"

Planned Parenthood
pulls the shutters.

November 20, Flagstaff, nothing

here's that rainy day
I'd been hoping for
door open on the lot
cold mountain wind
highway 17 rush
of autos & ringing
ears of rock & roll
cuties in a sack
bananas looking hurt
my suitcase, homesick
underwear & socks
waiting obediently
in the laundry hoping
against abandonment
not the first time

my breaths short
could be deadly
reading Edward Dorn
loading the car
with tired hopes
music is eternal
optimism said Jerry G
Woody's thousands of
songs in notebooks
seen the other day
by myself in Tulsa
gave birth to this land
it's our land & we all
need something to plow.

Quiet night at home in the 6

room 106 of the Flagstaff Motel 6
a cozy night in for a musician
wall-heater fan overdrive
drys me like a pelt
the world right outside my door
downtime after eleven shows
driving mad across Indian Lands
Oklahoma, New Mexico, Arizona
the earth cries out for blood spilled
orange sports car burnt shell in a dusty yard
random wheels farm tools rolls of paper
trash demobilized outlaws & tax cheats
ancient white church on a dry mud rise
with no roof bare to the blues skies
criss cross chem-trails over Indian casino
I walked through the truckstop breathless
caffeine & water & pain relievers
screaming sports moron broadcast from LA
a cannon blast of blah blah blah
with Black Crows drummer who doesn't know
where the cities are they're playing

later, millennium hippie boy & girl hitching with sign
for Sedona girl says hi to me the boy nothing
students wear high boots cut dashing figures
scarves leather chewing gum acne
did I really see the "Raul Castro Library?"
had a bad dream last night — T-Bone
thought he was God & needed dissuasion
official Arizona state roadside sign
bears Japanese sun death symbol
from World War Two traditional
nazi arms of dying son on the cross
& Satan is the name of the lawman here.

But at least I'm catching up
on my exhaustion!

Little Rock Coffee

Leather armchairs in a circle
filled with travelers who never meet eyes
while silly little white girl voices
sing dooby-dooby pop dribble
    via sonic ventilation system:

"there must be something in the water
    to make me love you like I do."

Room 107 pt 2

sleepless I switch on light to read about Purgatory but end up
scribbling in red notebook two more weeks of one-nighters
then fly home Thanksgiving Eve Love Field to SFO the plan
anyhow sheltered at the 6 in Dallas digging the ringing in my
ears the 5 ay em constant whir & rumble Doplar symphony of
roar & slowly falling tones of the race outside — everybody's
behind & I need sleep.

my suitcase open on the floor like the top of a ladder-way to
the underworld — my hat a basin by the bed the other side
of which is untouched my guitars propped like begging dogs
at the table the basics — a door on a parking lot — dirty
yellow curtain — bedspread like a seasick Hawaiian shirt
orange & blue — microwave robots head above the waist-high
refrigerator awaits commands flashing yesterday's time & I'm
choosing to stay calm.

Motel 6

up in the dark
thru passing ropes of traffic noise
off the I-35 frontage road near Dallas
rising then falling bass tones the occasional
satellite orbits like Hendrix — room 107
this afternoon the Indian woman
very black eyes barked answers to my queries
Dallas is only her latest home now I understand
leaving the lights on for americas el cheapo
travelers one star in the black sky
deformed blurry white moon — the toilet belongs
in a space capsule too — sheeshing the yellow
splashes instantly — the fan's music a chord
I'm typing this in the dark
it's four fourteen ay-em

At the Beef & Ale House, Buffalo, 1971

We were lucky to get a table
in the smoky dark
Friday night at the Beef & Ale
the band is on the floor
   up front
with their backs to
   Buffalo's Main Street
A medieval tavern
& the jukebox blares
   the Isley Brothers
It's hot in here
   tho' a blizzards outside
no matter-- the musicians
   on their break
grab their coats & hit the door
   out into the snow

Stan Szelest is the rock 'n roll king
   in this here smoke-belching steel town
the bridges rust for him
the rivers freeze
   the way he wants them to freeze
the street-drags under the skyway
   are done for the season
the ghetto shimmers with dirty ice
garbage men wrap scarves
   around their chops
knock their frozen gloves together

& the band plays three sets
stops at two
rock & roll piano
honky tonk beauty
   of snow on red brick
   & broken cobblestones
the piano has a taste of whiskey
   & a Genesee chaser

Marvin Gaye is on the Seabird
  & Honky Tonk Woman
  --the song that changed everything
  for Ernie--he played it
  a thousand times
  on his Telecaster
but Stan's fingers hammer blues trills
  & roll out of the black & white
& his left hand is the light
  on the porch

outside
the car turns over finally
  & so as not to freeze again
  they leave it running in the lot
& come back into the club to listen
& dig the girls with long thick black hair
pouring back over their shoulders
covered in brown leather with
tough talk & cigarettes
  dangling from sweet lips

the wars on the tv over the bar
  with the sound turned off
black leather jackets & gloves
dark & warm tones of jeans
the black & blue of the Buffalo night

The band is back
the drummer kicks it in
& it's loud — the kind of loud that
cuts right through to the bone
the other guitar player is skinny too
with huge Hendrix hair
plays a red Gibson like BB King's
& rocks his body on his heels
his mouth half smiling
eyes watching the crowd
watching the drummer

most of all his eyes go to Stan
who bobs & moves over the Wurlitzer
    like a fugitive
not one glance at the band
    from him
(that would strike fear!)
& he's singing now the one
    about the Mystery Train...

"Songs of the Nerves — Beat — & Plimsouls"

Seattle: after the first rehearsal: a long noisy slog through the
tunes & arrangements: my ears are ringing like air raid sirens.
Really beat, an 8 hour jam.

Music like a truckload of springs & trumpets
fanfare frantic pinned together
   at the elbows
stripped the hair
   right off my   eardrums
a call in the cold rain
dry throats in the downpour   stomping shoe leather
   insect treble/clammed beats
old mr menace
   strangles his happiest melody
   spit & chokes
the minutes   seem like ours
   days seem like
   my bone's outta joint

death letter anxiety

locust breath tension

liberty.

Lost track of the good word
   on the tube
     glow sound
     bullet generation
     replaced by calisthenics
     pleas turned to
     role transmission

mechanics not music
  awkwardly cut off at the knees
  out of syncopation.
Bound to get better tomorrow!

Vancouver

pine trees in the rain
headlights & brightly lit cloud screen
going to our first show

rain has stopped
snow piled at highway side
first day of the third month

Iron Road

the sound guy with the handlebar mustache
takes a header off the riser
  on my side falling hard
feet-up into the stage-side pit.
  climbs out himself
  "you ok?" "oh yeah–fine"
later falls over onto the merch table
  in the lobby several times.

a kid in a watch cap
  army surplus jacket
  who has possibly never shaved
  comes up close & promises me
  with a straight eye-to-eye look:
  "I used to follow you guys
  in 1978!"

Human collection circus — sinking eyes look away — no
words
  spoken — tho' tension feels like a viral infection: wound up
  wires ringing with anger. Retreat of a friendly adversary,
  not always a good omen — Elvis used to "get his shoulders
up"
  brooding — the quiet evil — real pain & fear--option.

"The show will be morally good"
  so said the Carter Family & Hank
  now again for a muddle of
  mustachioed 'teens'
  beyond 'extreme' & "in your face"
  & 'edge' finally.

"eat your Maypo, brats!"

"A gig inside a beer can"

Lee & I raise our palms to the lightbulb — feeling the heat from
across the room — kids in denims — combat boots — blue
hair & army jackets w/ epaulets — many wounded for decora-
tion — or from battle & disease of punk rock millennium — while
the musical lava flow — rolling surf — 2 boys & 2 girls on
stage — make a ragged & rugged soulful band — the bass player
with long dark hair & green sneakers as I come off stage earli-
er — he collars me — "I'm going to tell you the wildest story
you ever heard" — well he did tell me some nonsense about a
coincidence — "you were dating her sister in 1983!" -- but he's a
rocker — from London, Ontario -- across the bridge from De-
troit -- the Detroit toughness & style & rock'n roll is everything like
Lauran from the Dogs — Lindy --- his lead singer the whole place
was shipwrecked.

Lee

"Gigs that are way up stairs are always fucked up gigs!" says Lee
afterward, with his hard won teenage rock & roll highway knowledge.
"The gigs that are hard to get into" & people sleeping there &
smoking — the bands playing loud & hard — heard in hallways
through huge & thick doors rehearsing the most intense formulations
of fast moving metal sculpture terror & aggression — hanging mad
shapes — like a knife fight or deadly high speed maneuvers.

The floor of the place, afterwards covered in bottles, cups, wrappers,
soggy flyers, spilled liquid.

(end of the day at the tour stop)

the tv clatters
like a horserace announcement
  an hysterical neighbor
  on pain-relief
the boys in the group
  lay about like victims
  horizontal hombre collection
  lives in procession
my foot is running on red
  an ache comes in
  through the floor
  with the heat of magma
familiar music sounds strange
  after this afternoons tonal struggle.

I'm far far far from home
  exit for Canada tomorrow pm.
that dream last night wasn't so good
  secret surveillance & a league of
  hidden enemies
  but today's work came in a crowd
  set off smoke bombs & whistles
  amazement from the pulpit

the windows blinked — hard to recall what I was
  & what I was doing before
  I risked my rocket to save you
  play your anthem & stay with you
  along
  a long
  highway
  corrupted by
  a bitter compass.

the club in Seattle

far western — pacific feel — checkerboard asbestos floor —
the emotional chess we play — 29 dates to go — the girls Chelsea
& Justine show — Summer Twins — with Danny and Marsio —
at the start of the show my own guitar & voice are so loud in the
floor monitor it makes me dizzy

(girl in the middle of the crowd surge — digging the show —
nodding & smiling until the moshers dervished over
& collided with her — she heaved backbone ten fold twice —
sent whole numbers of them flying & that was the end of it.)

mad task

who sent you
   to open windows
   on the rolling train?

sand walker
lurching messenger
your guitar is an off brand
   "made in china by a
   12 year old"

the rest of the equipment is borrowed
   from young girls
& the guy helping carry — that volunteer
has just come back from
   a pepper spray holiday up state

good thing
   the road has taught you trust

Portland, city of youth

rivers bridges punk rock coffee skullcaps kids everywhere
& twenties but our gig in red brick curtains blue & red lit
burlesque theater now rock palace we see our name atop
shining white marquee but the show is weary as the sound
disintegrates — strings break & the kids don't come but go to
punk show down the street & we have a little crowd that never
really ignites but I'm flatfoot — my vocal cords torn. At best we
manage a draw — or we lose on points is more like it. My body
aches like I've been playing football---my spine & the backs of
my legs. Now it's 8:45 a.m. & I can't sleep so I write this in the
days a.m. — grey light through hotel room curtains in room
while Amos & Lee sleep in the next bed.

HW 5

like the background of an Italian Renaissance painting--mountains
against distance--mist--strange buildings. Sunset — the bareness
of the late winter--shades of gold & brown — sun over my right
shoulder--hand casting sharp shadows on the page as I write--the
orchards in rows & the bare fields--South of Gilroy nearly 5pm--semi-
trucks in lines on both sides of freeway. Mounds almost like barrows
heading up in foothills to mountains.

Olive orchards & black cattle feeding & the men inside the dark van
tell tales of deception & outrage — anger & innocence "fear + hope
are: vision" — Blake's equation.

March 8 – south to San Diego – van
(after SF & LA shows)

empty street — windy asphalt — parking lot to the stars — non-catchy pop on the jukebox — shotgun seat watching Orange Kingdom rewind past the "fires of Wilmington" American flag refinery hell — by day a jumble of tubal pollution — pockets of filth & foul decay behind your tongue & corrupted eyes — red cranes — unfinished bridge showing it's ribs — convertible dreamers — routine anger

insults & long weeks of dirty rags in the pit of solar plexus — shrivelled foreskins of thought — dream fists — bile corrosive — a chain of gigs like stops on a prison train & what are the hours on stage worth?

pacific ocean blue — walking on water means trouble — nuclear breasts of machine frenzy & the border check like a hose depot—the sea no longer the fantasy focus of my freedom—a western edge where no road goes through.

San Diego Sensations

Cali-Mexican wildness of the street
   & trees shrubs grass & birds
fellaheen — loose & jumbled
   seek-a-level sprawl
packed club midnight
   but a deadline drain emptiness

Dinosaurs still roam
   in El Cajon
there are still sword fights
   on Normal Heights
the jolly roger still flies
   in the harbor skies
where the jets land between the buildings.

land of the endless grind
land of tinselated sunshine
land of the empty pickup

candy colored radio babel
the false bottom of a mixed bag
stop & go doubletalk
   at fingertip ease
but now the fingers are burning
   everybody's got a sore throat
   snipers fire on the tennis club
   the swat team responds
   with the brickbats of pollution & belief

I used to live here now I'm passing through
I used to gargle radioactive surf
   in the King Kong brine
   now it's bottled fuji
   at the desert airport.

Leaving Austin North on 35

overcast oncoming with headlamps
on — heart's got a funny beat & my
left foot is cauliflower–excedrin
E's swimming in the alimentary
canal — silence from the back
seats — who knows what terrible
ordeals of crankiness plus
power-drive endured by these
brave band mates — people don't change
or they won't — but you can change how
you take it — if you want.

"Burger Heaven"

seven shows — forty eight hours
a cross town traipse with equipage
to boot — Austin sixth street SXSW
It's Mardi Gras minus the purpose — the soul
men dressed as flashlights
dancing down the middle of a blocked
off street — from a huge mad teenage
Burger Records teens & 20 something gig
at 29th street Spider House coffee joint
500 kids Bill Murray — someone says
"someone who wants to meet you"
& it's him "saw you guys last night
at the Continental–I dig what you're doing!"
me & Bill Murray facing each other packed
into the chaos — I say something like
"what do all these kids want with the nerves?"
& "these Burger kids are the future of rock + roll"
& to answer he makes a motion with his right
hand, of sticking in a key & twisting
it to the right, hard—he does this
twice—then comes up on stage — following
me up—to introduce us—which started
a screaming rockin' set—that included
a broken string on my axe, stage
diving audience members & the whole
place singing the lyrics to
(the Nerves song) when you find out
spontaneously.

..after counting my bills & doing the math

I wept for Buddy Holly who played his last gig in the Surf
Ballroom where I sit now & write this as they play the film---he
had to tour on murderous "winter dance party" substandard
gigs 'cause Norman Petty wouldn't pay Buddy's royalties — an
attempt to control Buddy, bring him back into line — so he hit
the road in unheated bus in the dead of winter storms.

I don't want to see the crash site — their songs could fly but
the sky wouldn't hold them---the place where a dream crashed
& died---no I don't want to see it---it could be anywhere-the
ballroom was another matter---the ghosts still walk the stage---
the payphone---the dressing room---the ticket booth.

Surf Ballroom

the ghosts shine on shellac
stage boards tremble--the flag
coughs-- a phone booth pulls its
collar--the tables & tradewinds
shamble--Buddy Holly is & he's
back in town--landing well on
the roof worked out this time
telegraph fingers softened & tapped
a dovetailed melody of change
in the clouds of snow
& no field was his graveyard.

phantom--peering over the
drums Buddy's backbeat for
Dion & the Belmonts--shades & a
suit & later his Stratocaster
freezing by day--subzero by night
they brought the soul & sound of
America-- "it's called rock & roll"
& the people are sweetly
smiling--instead of causing wars as
grimaced hotheads & love is sweet
& you can tap your feet.

apparition lingers over pay
phone--last call home--last
dressing room--last stage-the end
came like a Monday morning
melody joy friendship spirits
flying in the great beauty of
the holy ballroom--anyone
can fall to the ground & die
in a storm but with the right
music anyone can fly & landings
take care of themselves.

Death you thief—where'd you
take them? Richie Valens could
levitate a room–did somebody say
it was OK? Temptations? Asbestos
tiles polished to a shine—stairs
swinging on ropes from the
ceiling—girls in long dresses
& hairdo's & soft beautiful
flesh & shining eyes
for your fingertips—gentle beast
love flowers — roaming with children.

St. Paul

the St. Paul all night railroad
car diner on the corner — you go in at
1a.m. & the man with the red nose—in white
pants shirt cap—behind the cluttered counter
says "what?" after every order
throws the cups—everything's tossed off
"the other guy will ring you up"
"what?' with a squint — out in
the street–trouble brewin' up
the passing car shoots a "faggot"
our way–people here are working
out big problems–their tattoos
are itching.

March 26 Chicago

a Sunday night crowd — early show — dark club — 150 or so folks
including Allen, long time fan with the pompadour — friend from
LA — a bit older than me–always used to be with Heather — they've
split now — and he says 'many friends have died!' Mary Beth
B. — friend of the midsummer Nerves tour 1977 — I met her &
stayed at her house for a couple weeks always liked her — met her
mom for God's sake! well she's a grandmother now…grey hair down
her back, came with her man & she plays music — well I knew she
always did — she's proud to say she still does "for fun" — I didn't
recognize her at first. She went to get me some water & I asked her
name — "Mary" she said but I didn't get it. But then she said her full
name & I knew & said "of 3344 N. Wolcott!" & she laughed & said
'yeah.' It was nice to see her–-just to say? We're alive! Perilous human
situation after years & all you can do is be present — see people with
your eyes open–stay in the present & it all comes alive–-the music
must be played in this state, when the lights go out the people go
home–-fires attract…wolves.

St. Paul II

the worst part was the yelling,
the in-your-face-drama for nothing
& finally the drunken call out
   —-no can do!
So now the chips are falling
   & draw the line
people can do what they want
   & think best.

I'm in the dark about so much.
Just like you.
So keep eyes & ears open
   steer — try to help — stay cool.

Hammond 7 Chicago 25

On the 90 past the Gary/Chicago airport
a little strip out here in the poison fields
telephone & power lines march to sci-fi horizon
road storage bins white but rusted
jumbles of bridges, stacks & fields of bush
electric train blue skies chilly — not clouds but tinge
   of white wood frames & highway
   trash up on the embankment

Calumet Avenue—Chicago Skyway — cell phone towers
   & round storage tanks
   cat tails on the side of the road
   swamps & in the distance — cranes
   steel towers of industry
   piles of junk & a school by the storage depots
   tank trucks & a bridge over the water's gun-metal blue
   "give you 50 bucks to drink a glass of that swill!"

Way off see industrial slopes
   church steeples in another direction
we're listening to the Misfits
   & see wind mills—futuristic white
   & a cement factory.
   smell rank & sulfurous
   red & white stacks atop reddish block building
   set at an angle over ancient belt conveyors
   & there's the lake—trains of empty coal bins lined up
   on the track as the skyway climbs above—NS freight
   steel bridge tops & a small boat harbor of jammed-in
masts
   under weird black steel tower with shack atop
   & mechanical wheels

This amazing wilderness strip of industrial land on the
Calumet

& 'the confederate space program"
rooftop watertowers (old joke)
everywhere train tracks 3 or 4 wide--BNSF cars
There's Chicago now — across the fields to the North.

& right in the middle of all this industrial chaos, the projects.

Mountains of Northern New Mexico

Snow covered top & sides
   & the wheeling space that fascinates me
pines cover the rocks & sand & desert earth
   'neath the biggest blue sky
26 miles from Albuquerque
   truckers & pick up drivers
   shack villages by the side of the road
   with sports cars parked outside

& a sign says "Zuzax 1 Mile."

That motel room was so cold
   me & Lee sleeping — trying to anyway
   I thought my feet were wet — the covers were flimsy
   the heat wasn't working just blowing cold air
I'd nod off then wake up from the cold
   & ended up putting on my jacket over a t & shirt
   & my jeans & pajamas & underwear
2 pairs of sox & finally get up at 10am.

New Mexico — endless trains
   the double e & red cliff mesas
   & Navajo chants on the radio
Road side service station with tires holding the roof down
New Mexico ramshackle daily — make it up as we go along
   double wide nation
Beautiful hymn on Navajo Christian radio broadcast
   solemn with piano
   from deep tones to high children's voices
   & simple silver chords.

"Continental Divide 1 Mile" & Indian village market.

And on the Arizona border
   clay cliffs, a winding river
   & we're right up on the mesa now,
   with train tracks between us the river & the cliffs

freight rolling on the left—-empty cars
we're in Arizona now coming down out of the glow
   & soon into the golden whiteness of the sun
   the pale blue & fields of green — California!

We've returned
it's been 6 weeks on the road
Los Angeles 448 now — the signs down?
& into the clear — mountains ahead & to the north

We've got Spiritualized on the player
   in their late night cathedral rock & roll glory

So, we did it: 972 miles today, 870 yesterday
   Toledo to St Louis — by way of Milwaukee day before that,
   & from Collinsville, Connecticut to Toledo, the first day.

Made it home to Los Angeles
   for my 58th Birthday
   --got in April 5 at 1am.

Rockabilly Moon 1977

Everybody got drunk
one sip at a time
she wasn't looking
anymore than I was
& I was playing bass
in the Nerves
It was the month of May

We were up in the Rockies
playing Denver on tour
the gig was upstairs & over
a record store called Wax Trax
Jim was still alive then
in fact, he was in his prime
& he threw a great party
in the store & everybody came

Records played non-stop
"flying saucers rock and roll"
"my gal is red hot" "red headed
  woman'" & "gloria"
"be my baby"
I took a ride with her
& a shower at her place
& nearly had a heart attack

So she went to cop speed
from her dentist friend
she went in for 15 or 20
minutes & came out with some
"amphetamine sulphate"
a huge bottle that pretty much
took care of me for the rest
of the summer I mean life

Up in the blue rockies
pine trees & altitude
air charged & crackling
the threat of huge storms
seen from fifty miles across
rock & rockabilly records
free beer the first batch
of great punk rock singles

& a cast of twenty or thirty
rockers drinking from the keg
while the records played
I read about Spector
feeding my imagination
& musical questions
ambitions & big ideas
a song Rockabilly Moon

A photographer, Patti
took the band's picture out front
& we said goodbye to Denver
& took off on many adventures
but we came back & dropped in
on our return trip to California
two months later — broke & hungry
to sell the Ramones shirts
off our backs, for gas money.

Ace Of Spades 2014

home for a few weeks
inside — with the furniture
& the black terrier hopping up
at least he smells
like a dog
should smell

venetian blinds down
my ears ringing
sirens from the firehouse
rumble of firetrucks
but no story — no adventure
cut off cold
purple blanket pulled up
over my legs & chest
feet in pain from cold
my books
Bolano & Santiago
old Hit Paraders on the piano
guitar propped against a couch

Lou Reed died last night.

cut off from my muse
cut off from adventure
cut off from the feelings
the memories.
cut off
from the songs, the music
the quickening feeling
the burn in my chest
the blues
cut off--
most of my life cut off.
shut down--buried
all the wasted
days years decades

where are the songs?
poetry? novels?
books?
Day off/cut off
I'm my own jailor.
fear is my cell
words never spoken
stories I can't tell.

Tumbleweed Hillside 1985

High in Laurel Canyon
owl on the telephone line
snake on the ground
raccoon in the trashcan
   it's late sunset
The sun has gone down.
lights are coming on
across Los Angeles
& I'm just beginning to see
what I've done to myself.

Where's my band?
where are my pals?
I'm on my own now.

In the heat waves
we had a good laugh
but all my particular good times
   are desperate
I needed you so bad
at least it's over
   now — thank God.

War protest 1970

We heard the clang
& shout of the riot
floating in the cold
october atmosphere
nostrils bitten by sweat
sweet & bitter taste dead
summer green now dry
& golden the scent
gunpowder too & teargas
across the cold courtyards
stone edifices with eyes shut
government
the fortress of everyday life
in the city we were scared
& excited to be so close
history going down
but when they came
around the corner
we got a good look
at myriad, the riot beast
roaring, angry in a mob
terrified we cut out the side
up main street just as
the masked man on a bicycle
threw a fire bomb through
the window
of the bank & split

Then the sedan raced up
& four large men in suits
got out & threw us
up against the car.

Along For The Ride 1990

yes this is over, too
her sprung hair
   under the green fluorescents
my orange vest
   over the brown & white check
under that barbed electric field
in the converted disco showroom
of a half-filled night club
somewhere in New Jersey

let's face up: I was dressed
   like a Christmas tree
I was still thin & had given up
speed
   & smokes

She stood & glared
at the line of well-wishers
   who had just engaged their kicks
in my musical concert
maybe she was furious
   because I was giving
   my attention away
   while she was there.

I'd never seen that club before
   nor since.

We had a shouting match
   on the New Jersey Turnpike
I was so angry.
lines of traffic under the floodlights
   at the toll-booths.
was it pissing rain that evening?
or was that running world,
   that dripping sinking mess
   I couldn't see through —
      only a child's tears?

Born liar I've found.
I just won't call.
 the door could be locked or frozen
 the fruits in the hamper are fresh or faded
 your eyes are pretty, gimlets, razor cuts
 love is a slash against a wall
 even the daylight has been conned & bothered
 twisted & turned for Babel-chuck.

Born liars are made men
 fliers in todays air-force.

Hear that semi grindin' gears up the grade?
That's my sound, baby!
Hear the motor-sickle music of tough cough rumble-lators?
That's my sound
    'cause I'm a migged up memory bank
    of lonesome jewels, staggered skylights
    peppered stakes & alpha-bone belittlement.

Sound, it's all about sound, crack, dag, whiffle.
Barby, skydog, poof! Tinkly dinkly crang-dozers
    of sprinkle beat ax-drops.

Hear it? Mine.

Trusty critter
    casts off a wave
    of nosegays
hotrods race
    on the river road
Chet & the chums
    are heading for the old
        Ame's place, abandoned
        but for the gangland cuties.
Frank & Joe sweat it
escape & jerk profusely
    with ex-cops.
Treasure, pleasure, it's all radium.

Critic's squint
snakes ameliorate
    the gargoyle
serpents pay by the head
extra-crispy pants walk
    the main line
        pass on the right
        finger their zippers
the critter rolls and sighs.

"Her old man's in prison
    but he's cool with it."

Newcastle.
My friend
I'm lonesome tonight
in this cheap hotel
a room far from home
listening to the church bells
counting their tones
bong, bong, bong, bong.
The birds don't know
   if it's day or night.

I wish I could sleep
   but ghosts do calisthenics
   by the bed.
The previous tenant left his marks:
   used tea cups & towels
   soap bar in the sink.
There were only 20 at the show
   & they didn't love me,
   no shouts, no encore.
But afterwards,
   everybody said 'You were great!'

Red blinking light
    exhausted sentinels voice
    like a river, a radio, a ribbon
      & a road.
Help me, clown-man.
I'm delayed by a spastic ponce
dogs in devilment, crows.
I'm mud, silting to the bottom.
The bed remains.
    A board of raftdom, a rack

A vacation in Barbezonian splendor.

"Help me, Mick, ok?
I'm dyin' over here.
I need a hit more
    than Queenie
      needs a jukebox dime."

In the beach side room
  with the pom girl
the flag used me for a blanket
the myriad overhead
  & the poverty within & without
 the pseudo cowboy's voice
  on the sound system — onions & garlic.

Smooth & long creamy
  & rolls compliant. The radio drone
  the palm frond rustle. The dinner bell.
The time like a razor wound.
The end of the good life
  was a long time ago. A fish jumps
  a mile outside, it's a marlin, a young fish
  an impossible force.

Garlic & onions. Celery.

It's been a week now
   of automatic doors, stale odours
   trains & plains, sky-toppers
   faces in front & waters in back.
Anxiety balances on a nail, the whole dark
   brick night set to topple & scream
   collapsed to room size & a bare ceiling bulb
but I'm protected by the power of prayer,
   by you & by love.

My mind wanders & some nights
   never comes home. The heat shuts down
   & the bodies go cold. Stadiums are no place
   for pearl-divers fog lamps. Gasoline flows
   in the gutter, sandwiches go on strike.

Paralyzed faces & fingers on fruit loops
   piles of dollars on airplane wings
   giggle & shout & court the teens
   bless the frozen bones, the rising pleas
   the toxic touch of a foreign prince.

O suffer these tears, quagmire.

Coolant required.

It hurt but now it's over
the lights on plasticine
skin stretched on wires,
flood lights & heats
trained on powder puffs
midgets & trance doctors.

The train pulled out
& it was the whole world
disappearing
across the universe
& I get on board.

A Kodak moment
before & after the Grail.
fleas in a corporeal sunset
& sacrifice to the god
the trophies were passed to the front
& tossed into the hole
right before we all jumped.

Hoops billy-roved my targrave steed
  & nestled plump round a tin gloss window
Weather incensed & multi-coloured
  poured over the sheep coats
  the head-down grazers
  & anxious swallows & squirrels.

Up again & rested as the sun falls
  the river rolls, time drips & drops
  I'm myself & who else?
Recuperation is daily, on a very short rope
  & it's nailed to my heart.
Books are comfort. A warm, well lit lonely
  & carpeted room, between the beds
  on the floor, the drawers are breathing
  friendly, the bath a casket, sleep a death
  & now I'm reborn clean, on another highway.

I was nailed to a stick & lifted above the crowd
a clown among clowns, an inflatable fool
nose glowing like a painful red pepper & cheeks rouged.

The orchestra played & I was forced to dance
no one fired bullets at my feet
the stage was simply heated & I jumped

The ceiling ripped open by a magic hook on a chain
which was passed through my solar plexus
& I was lifted out, to the great relief of all.

In the movie Homeboy, Micky Rourke
plays a washed up boxer,
punch drunk, on the way down

but everytime the going gets rough
he smiles like a child, from the eyes
an untroubled carefree look
while they beat the crap out of him.

From here on I smile too
every time the gloves come out or off
anytime I'm scared
whenever I get hit
'cause I'm not going down no more either.

Spent the morning casting gems
   at Shakespeare & walking green
   like a wayward child.

This explains my aversion to Chinese hats
   dancing naked in traffic
   & sipping gutter water
      with a straw.

Laughing mouths — teeth broken
   on the gravel — this is known as
   the 'Liar's Celebration'

But I'm shy & miss my chances
   especially when
   they're not chances at all.

Nerves of steel, they set up a smudge
　　on the prettiest block of green.
Black towers & clouds over the trees
　　at the end of the fields. The people bore up
　　like pack rats, moved down to the seaside
　　inebriated on cheap twaddle & bowl foam,
　　or gargling fine wines.
Noel poured his pants full of nuclear steam
　　history erected itself & there were horses
　　at the ends, taxis beyond & a fool prince

They're turning the heat up under me again
  but I'm no junkie, no drunk
  I pay as many of my bills as I can

Sure, I work on the road
  take care of my sick Mother too
  but I'm just tryin' to make my way
  nobody's gon' take care of me

Except you, Biggie.

Denise, many the little sheepy-sheeps
   gaze contentedly on the sunlit fields
   & the North Sea, grey & white capped
   & rolling off the end of the rolling hills.

We could live here & be satisfied ourselves
   in love, with what's left of each other
   & the world, as the sky blue clouds gather
   for a sea voyage. Dark lights on the water
   & way out yonder a craft we won't betray

& we'll live in our dreams, giant.

www.ingramcontent.com/pod-product-compliance
Lightning Source LLC
Chambersburg PA
CBHW072041040426
42447CB00012BB/2963